# How To Complete A BPO

## The Complete Guide to Broker Price Opinions

Jonathan Eldrige

# Disclaimer

The following information is provided for information purposes only. Our opinion is given based on our experience and not to be considered legal or professional advice. Please consult with a qualified attorney, tax accountant, and other professionals to ensure you are proceeding correctly. Our information is provided as an opinion of our experience and we do not warrant, represent, or provide any guarantees as to the suitability or outcome you may have.

We reference and link to third party services. Some of these third party links are affiliate programs or may be affiliated companies of the publisher that we may be compensated for in the event you sign up. The use of these third party services does not guarantee any success and or earnings for your business. Furthermore, we do not guarantee any information, instruction, or opinion of these products or services. Readers are advised to do their own due diligence when deciding on a suitable company or fit for their business needs.

Readers of this book agree that Certatim, LLC, all officers and owners are not responsible for the success or failure of your business decisions related to any information provided in this book.

# Table of Contents

Functional Utility

Heating and Cooling or Energy Efficient Items

Garage and Carport

Porches, Decks, Patios, Balconies, Pools, Fireplaces, Fences, Lions and Tigers Oh My.

Repairs

Marketing Strategy and Comments

Market Value

Photos

## What is a BPO

BPO is an acronym for Broker Price Opinion. Broker Price Opinions are an easy way for a third party to get an objective opinion of value from a Real Estate Professional. A BPO typically requests multiple values from the individual performing the report, for example an as is and repaired value. It is often commonplace to request an estimate of time required to sell a property. BPO's are most often completed for the present time, however, it is not out of the ordinary for a request for values on specific dates in the past. As the name BPO implies, Real Estate Professionals (brokers and/or agents) typically complete the reports. BPO's are a quick and less expensive alternative to a full-blown appraisal.

## Who Orders or Requests a BPO

A BPO can be ordered by a wide array of people, however, the most common requestor of a BPO is the owner of a property or a party that has a vested interest in a property. Banks, Mortgage note holders and Mortgage Insurance Companies are the most common parties requesting BPO's. Often times they have taken back a property through foreclosure and want to get an unbiased opinion of the current property value. Banks often order a BPO when reviewing proposed offers for short sales. A short sale is transaction where the bank agrees to sell the property for less then what is currently owed to them on the mortgage. If the bank believes that the mortgagor may default on their loan or that the cost to foreclose and then sell the home is greater than the loss of selling the home at the with the short sale value, the bank will typically accept a short sale. During the approval process the bank employs Real Estate Professionals to provide an independent third party opinion of the current market value to assist in negotiating an offer they have received on a home. The bank wants to ensure the offer is for at least a fair market value.

In addition to banks or note holders, there are often estate liquidations, bankruptcy valuations, divorce settlements and a myriad of other reasons that a property owner may want to receive a third party unbiased opinion of the market value of a home.  A BPO is a commonly used simple tool to get this value.

With all of these potential sources of BPO business now is as good a time as any to get started performing for fee BPO's.

**BPO vs Appraisal**

You may wonder what's the difference between a BPO and an Appraisal and why wouldn't people just hire an appraiser to get a valuation of the property. Appraisals are the industry standard when underwriting new loans on purchases and refinances, but in light of the dramatic increase in mortgage defaults, BPOs have become extremely popular.  The cost of a BPO can range depending on whether the property is Residential or commercial, whether it's rural or easily accessible, and whether the Broker is doing an interior or exterior BPO. (More on that later) Regardless of the variations in costs of different types of BPOs, they are generally speaking far less expensive ranging from $40 - $300 or so based on the factors previously mentioned. Most appraisals will begin at $250 and can go as high as $5000 based on those same factors.

Appraisers are often guided by strict guidelines and state mandated rules that do make an appraisal more thorough and more regulated. Whether this results in a more accurate valuation or just a more regulated one is up for debate. Appraisals often take longer to complete and generally in the range of a week, BPOs are often ordered and returned in 3 to 4 days. With the increased cost and often longer deliver timeframes, Banks and other interested parties have started putting more focus on BPOs as opposed to Appraisals in many situations. Ordering a BPO often allows them to get a quick opinion of market value multiple times over the course of 6 months. Given the higher cost of an appraisal a BPO is often the best choice to keep an eye on the change in value and market conditions.

**Interior or Exterior BPO**

When receiving an order for a BPO it's important to note whether it is an interior or exterior BPO. An Exterior BPO is often referred to as a Drive-By BPO, and is just that. You will take photos of the exterior of the home and not actually make an appointment to see the interior of the property. In some cases banks order Exterior BPO's for properties where the occupant may not be aware that the BPO has been ordered. You should be careful when performing exterior BPO's as you may not always know the situation with the occupants. Take your pictures and be on your way. Exterior BPOs are less complete and comprehensive as you are valuing the property based solely on and outside assessment. Who knows what the condition is inside? You would make your adjustments assuming its average and note such.

An interior BPO is the more commonly ordered BPO and means that you will actually inspect the interior of the property. This gives you the ability to review the home and its layout, condition, flow and aesthetics. These factors help in providing a more comprehensive BPO but often may mean additional work with coordinating access the property. Often interior BPO compensation is more than Drive By or exterior BPOs, however, there is often more work required to complete an interior BPO as well.

**Making Money with BPOs**

When the market turned from boom to bust and residential and commercial sales volumes slowed in various regions of the country, many agents or brokers found themselves in a predicament and unable to continue to make a steady income. There was a dramatic increase in the number of loan defaults and foreclosed properties. Some agents moved into REO sales or Real Estate Owned sales, which is selling properties for the banks or other note holders. These brokers and/or agents were employed to sell the properties and mitigate any further loss on the loans. This industry became competitive quickly and agents were all racing to get into one of the few specializations within Real Estate that was still generating revenue.

If you were not interested in managing properties or maintaining them or could not obtain any of these REO clients then you needed to also consider other verticals to make revenue. Because there were and continue to be so many foreclosures and short sale properties, the use of BPOs became and continues to be extremely popular. Agents started signing up with various companies who offer BPOs for a fee. Some of these companies get large orders from institutional clients that they may have and agents can receive up to a dozen orders a day in some cases. These BPO's can pay on average of about $60, but it differs based upon the client, complexity, and time frame. Many agents focus entirely on BPO's and make a living solely from providing this service.

More common is the agent who supplements their commission income with a BPO order here or there or uses it to approve a pending sale they are working with. Many agents are unfamiliar with a BPO but may be listing a home for sale where the owner or note holder asks for a BPO to consider an offer they have received. While you may not be paid by the seller directly for the BPO, you can see how ultimately it is standing between you and your commission.

## What Makes up a BPO

BPOs come in different shapes and sizes but there are some elements that are almost always included in a BPO.  In order to arrive at a fair value for a property you need to make sure you have the facts about the property you are valuing, commonly referred to as the Subject Property.  BPO's will almost always include a detailed section for the Subjects characteristics and attributes.

Comparable properties are almost always included in an effective BPO to help obtain a fair assessment of the value of the property.  There are often 3 comparable sold properties and 3 comparable listed properties.  Comparable is subjective and is based on your opinion as a real estate professional that the property is as similar to the subject property as possible.  Some BPO's may require adjustments be made to reconcile the difference between the subject property and the comparable properties.

Conditions and Marketing recommendations are often a part of most BPOs.  The person ordering the BPO often wants to know the necessary repairs to the property, condition of the property and other recommendations for marketing of the property.  This is often detailed in a comments section.

Lastly most BPO's will ask for pictures.  They may want pictures of the subject property as well as pictures of the comparable properties used in the

BPO. The pictures may be exterior only or both interior subject photos and exterior photos.

## How to generate or Fill out a BPO

Many companies who order BPOs have their own systems they use and require you to enter your BPO into their web based system. Some of these formats are easier to use than others but if the provider has their own system you will need to enter your information into their system. Make sure to save often and regularly as you may lose internet connection at any time or get logged out accidentally. Nothing is more aggravating than to lose an hour or two of your data because of an internet outage. If you have not been asked to use a particular form or software you can head over to www.bpoforms.com . BPO Forms offers a number of different versions of BPOs and an easy way for you to adjust the information, save them and come back at a later time to print or email the completed form. Oftentimes banks or clients may come back and request information updated or changed and this allows you to easily make those changes. It's probably not such a good idea for you to try and complete a BPO using a word processor or some PDF typing or by hand. There are too many variables and changes that need to be made that you will easily waste more time than it's worth trying to accomplish it that way.

## The BPO Section by Section

It is important to know that many BPO's have different formats and often use different terminology interchangeably to describe different sections or fields.  In the following breakdown you will see terms that may differ slightly from the ones on your BPO.  Additionally various BPO formats exclude some sections outlined below and not all may be applicable to your format.

 The most widely used and accepted BPO format is the Fannie Mae Residential BPO form.  Fannie Mae is a semi-private company that is government sponsored and buys mortgages or pools of mortgages from private lenders.  Fannie Mae is the largest single issuer of single-family mortgage securities accounting for 48 percent of the market share at the end of 2013. Fannie Mae's purpose is creating liquidity in the residential lending marketplace. It accomplishes this through the purchase of mortgages that were originated by banks like Bank of America and Wells Fargo.

**Market Conditions**

An integral part of understanding the value of a property is understanding the factors that may effect this value.  The old adage of Supply vs Demand is no more relevant than in Real Estate. These market conditions ultimately affect how much someone is willing to pay for a property and how quickly it may sell.  Most BPOs have a section asking for current market conditions.  It is important to remember that they are looking for your professional opinion but it's impossible to have a 100% accurate number as the market is changing daily.  Do you believe the market conditions are slow or bullish, improving or excellent?  What is the overall sentiment towards purchasing and selling homes?  More importantly, what is the condition of the exact neighborhood where the subject property is located?

How are property values doing as a whole?  Obviously each property and pocket neighborhood has varying answers but on a whole what is going on with prices and time on market.  Are properties sitting on the market for longer periods of time and are prices decreasing as a result?  How are the employment conditions in the area?  Did the largest employer in town go out of business and was the local employment rate affected by the closure?   It is important to use generalizations when completing the marketing condition section of a BPO as you are trying to paint a picture of the local market in its entirety.  Not just a block or a gated community.

Sometimes a BPO requestor will want to know how many of the occupants are owners and how many are renters.  While this is not an exact science, you should be able to estimate the percentage of each based on your professional knowledge of the area.  Remember you have been hired to give your opinion as a market professional, whether they agree or not.  Knowing who the occupants are and the estimated breakdown is important to understand who a potential purchaser may be.  Is it likely an investor or an end user?  This information may help in determining how to market the property and whether or not repairs should be made. Primary residents may expect or prefer a fully renovated house whereas investors would be willing to purchase a property with more work required.

How much supply is in the current market? Is there an excess amount of inventory for sale now or is inventory at a normal level for the area? In addition to overall inventory, the BPO requestor may want to know how many of the homes are considered competition. If you are selling a single family home and there are only condominiums for sale then there isn't much direct competition. This may be a good or bad thing but an important part of giving an idea of the overall market conditions for the subject property. Does the area have foreclosed homes on the market or homes that are boarded up? Are the competing homes institutional or bank sales or investor sales or other primary residents?

It is important to remember that you know your market innately and that many of the people reviewing your BPO are often based in other States. They have no idea of the area or the feel or the community. You need to paint the picture for them through your report. Do not assume that the requestor knows anything about the area. It is actually helpful to assume the opposite. Answering the marketing condition questions helps give the requestor of a BPO an idea of the local area and other outside factors that may affect the value of the home.

## Marketability

Understanding the value of the property you are providing an opinion for (subject property) is largely based on the properties Marketability. How does the property stand in comparison to others? How does it compete with the others? Understanding how the property compares largely depends on the competition. While the market condition section provides an outline of the market as a whole, the marketability section relies on the actual subject property and its attributes.

Painting an accurate picture of the subject property's marketability starts with understanding the range of values for the current neighborhood. What price are homes selling for in this specific area? The marketability section provides a more granular look. The market conditions section requests information on a city-wide range while the marketability section focuses on the neighborhood.

Once you have defined the neighborhood values the BPO may ask where the property falls in comparison to other homes. Is the subject property over improved and the nicest house on the block? Is the subject property a tiny old home in a neighborhood where all other homes similar in age have been torn down to build new homes?

Marketing time, or the amount of time it will take to market a property, is a subjective question and as a real estate professional you may think that the marketing time is solely based on where a property is priced.  When this question is asked on a BPO, the requestor is trying to understand how long it is taking similar homes on the market to sell. Does it take a year for homes in this area to sell on average or is it more common for a home to remain on the market for 90 days.  This is your opinion and should be bolstered by reviewing average days on market in your MLS for that particular area.

Remember to remove your bias when completing a BPO. It is important to try and back up all of the information you provide with data. When there is no data available then fall back on your professional opinion.

An important part of a subject's marketability is the understanding of whether the property will qualify for financing.  Different types of loans have different restrictions and a conventional loan has much less stringent requirement than an FHA lender, which requires a stove and no active roof leaks or other health hazards. Requirements will also vary by geography.  As a professional you should be able to provide an opinion of whether the home will qualify for financing in its current state. If you remain unsure any number of local mortgage professionals would be more than glad to give you their opinion if you are not comfortable with the information.

Another important factor in determining the marketability of the property is researching the recent marketing activity on the subject itself. There is no better test to see if a property is marketable than to see if it was recently marketed. Was it listed and if so at what price? Did it ever go under contract? You can often take a look at the old Multiple Listing information for the subject property if it was recently marketed to get additional information. Maybe they are disclosing some information that is not visible from a precursory look but is integral to understanding the value. Did the property go under contract or sell and if not, why not? Was the property listed as a short sale? Does marketing a property as a short sale in this area affect the marketing timeframes? Remember this is just your opinion. Maybe you thought the property was overpriced or maybe it showed terribly and should have been painted to make it show better and buyers couldn't get past that.

The marketability section may also ask subject specific information. What type of home is the property? Here you will define if it's a town home or condominium or modular home. You may also need to define if the subject is a part of a homeowners association. Are their mandatory fees as a member in the association? Is it a condominium association or a homeowners association and what are the fees? Is there a master association, if so is the subject in a sub association within a master association. What's included in the fees? It is important to consider that the inclusions may have a large impact on the value of a property. If the association fees include cable television and internet access that may be a value to a homeowner of $200 a month. $200 a month equates roughly to mortgage payments on

$20,000 of financed home.  That's a substantial change in value.  An important consideration is the inclusion of insurance. Does the association handle the insurance of the structure?

## Competitive Listings or Closed Sales

The most important part of determining a property's value is to review what properties are currently for sale and what properties have recently sold.  There is no better indication of value than recent data of comparable homes.  If the house next door is twice the size of the subject property and is on the market or just sold that information is crucial in determining the value of the subject property.

The main principle guiding a BPO is the principle of substitution. In a perfect world you should be able to make adjustments in a BPO that would make the subject property a substitute for any of the comparables included on your report. Imagine a buyer is presented with two identical options, there should be no difference in which home they select.

Coming back to our example of the larger home next door to our subject. This may mean that you need to price the subject at a reduced price when compared to the larger home next door.  There are always exceptions to this rule.  You may say that maybe they don't want a larger home or the upkeep required. There is also a possibility that the larger home next door is an over improvement. Regardless, there is value to the additional square footage.  But these nuances are where you derive the market value of the subject property.  This is the most subjective portion of the BPO and it's important to understand that you are giving your opinion of how these factors may adjust the value of a home.  When providing an opinion on a BPO always try and provide as much data as possible to back up your argument.

## Selecting comparable properties

Selecting the appropriate comparable properties for your BPO is one of the most important and often most difficult steps of completing the BPO.  Without relevant comparable properties you are going to have trouble determining the value of the subject property.  Most BPO's will require 3 sold comparable listings, which should be sold within the last six months or more recent if possible and 3 active comparable listings.

In an effort to obtain 3 sold comparables and 3 listed comparables you should look for properties most similar to the subject property in all characteristics.  The same number of bedrooms, square footage, condition and characteristics across the street is the ideal comparable property.  Understanding that you won't find identical properties next door to the subject is fine but start with that as a baseline and slowly expand your criteria out to be more lax until you obtain the desired number of comparable properties.

The proximity of a comparable to your subject property is always an important factor. If the subject property is in a densely populated area you should be searching within a tighter radius. If the subject property is in a rural area you can expand your search radius more liberally.

You will adjust for the differences between the comparable properties and your subject property but the less variations you have the better the valuation will be. A perfect BPO would be one in which no adjustments would need to be made because all of the properties are identical to the subject property. This is unrealistic, but should assist you in selecting comparable properties that are as similar as possible to the subject.

## Making Adjustments to Comparables

One of the complexities in completing a BPO is making adjustments to the values based upon the differences in the properties. Some BPO's will not require adjustments. Most of the BPO's, especially the BPO's with higher fees will require you to make adjustments. Unless your comparable listings and sales are exact replicas of the subject property, you should be making adjustments.

Once you have selected your comparable properties, your next step is often adjusting the comparables item by item so that the ultimate value of each adjusted comparable price is an indication of the subject's property. NOTE: You will never adjust the price of the subject. All of the adjustments are always made to the comparable properties.  This can get confusing so let's look at some examples.

For simplicity we are going to look at two properties that are next door to each other in our fictitious world.  They are identical in every aspect including upkeep, presentation, color, bedrooms, bathrooms, exposure.  The only difference in the properties is that one has a pool and one does not.  That's the only difference.  This is where your professional opinion is important.

The question you are trying to answer here is what is the difference in value to the property based on the fact that the house has a pool.  It is important to understand that this is not the cost of building a pool.  The cost of building a pool may be $50,000, but certainly if the home just sold for $100,000 its fair to say that half the value of the home wasn't the pool.  Just because it costs a certain amount to add something to a home doesn't mean that's its fair market value when being sold as part of the home.  When purchasing a home the buyer is buying the home at wholesale value. In other words the buyer is buying the entire home in one piece, not the sum of all of its parts.

Consider yourself.  How much more would you be willing to pay for the home with the pool?  Maybe $10,000 or $15,000?  Maybe you don't want to have to clean the pool and think it's worthless but think about the majority.  The value is based on what you think the majority of people would value that difference.  Would most people be willing to pay $10,000 more for the property with the pool than the one without?

Now assuming we have settled on a $10,000 valuation for the pool, we need to make the adjustment now. We have mentioned before that you never adjust the value of the subject property so we need to make and adjustment to the comparable property to reflect the fact that the subject property does not have a pool. This will mean that we need to reduce the sales price of the comparable property by $10,000.

| | Subject Property | Comparable Sold 1 | Adjustments |
|---|---|---|---|
| Address | 123 Elm Street | 125 Elm Street | $0 |
| Sold Price | | $100,000 | |
| Square Feet | 2000 Square Feet | 2000 Square Feet | $0 |
| Bed/Bath | 3 Beds / 3 Baths | 3 Beds / 3 Baths | $0 |
| Pool / Deck | No Pool | Pool | -$10,000 |
| | | Adjusted Value | $90,000 |

The reason behind reducing the comparable property value by $10,000 is that we are trying to adjust the comparable properties so they are identical to the subject property. After the adjustments are made you should have a value which indicates the estimated value of the subject property. In this case we have agreed that some would be willing to pay $10,000 more for a house with a pool and in our case the comparable had a pool but the subject doesn't. To make the comparable property similar to the subject we would have to remove the pool or adjust the sold price by the amount someone would pay for the pool. When we subtract the $10,000 premium from the pool home we get $90,000.  This means that based on the pool being the only difference between these homes, our subject home has an estimated value of $90,000.

This can be complicated and many people struggle with these adjustments.  If you don't understand the reasoning or the math you can memorize the following acronyms to assist when completing a BPO.

## CIA – Comparable Inferior Add

## CBS – Comparable Superior Subtract

In our example the comparable had a superior condition of having a pool, (CBS) therefore we subtracted the value that we estimated for this condition.

When arriving at an adjustment value for your comparable characteristics, you should know that these values can differ based on the value of the home.  In the example above it may have been unfair to say that the value of the pool was $50,000 but consider two homes that were identical in every way except for a pool and the comparable property just sold for $750,000.  It's not farfetched to consider that having a pool or not in this scenario may have a $50,000 valuation adjustment to these comparables.  The value of adjustments may differ from property to property and no fixed formula can be used.  Your professional expertise and gut feeling is going to help you decide.

While making adjustments to the comparables is considered the most difficult part, the good news is that not all BPO formats require these adjustments. Some BPOs often ask you to just provide the most relevant comparable properties without making adjustments to the value. They may ask that you explain the differences in the properties from the subject property but not necessarily assign dollar values for these differences in prices. These are often quicker BPO's to complete but extra special attention should be given to selecting comparable properties most like the subject as you will not be adjusting the prices to factor in these differences.

**Proximity to Subject**

Your first factor is to make sure you are searching for homes in the same area as the subject. An ideal comparable is next door or across the street but that is typically difficult to find in most cases. You will need to expand your search to include an area that includes similar homes in a similar market condition. Proximity to the subject is often one of the best indicators of its comparability. If you are performing a BPO for a home in a particular community, try and keep the search to that particular community. If you are doing a valuation for a property in a condominium building then the most comparable properties would be located in the same condominium building. Furthermore, condominiums in the same line as the subject are the most comparable to the subject condo.

In principle, the further away the property is to the subject, the less like the property it is. In some cases you may be working with a rural farm area and homes are miles apart from one another. That is fine as long as you explain this and paint the picture that in order to obtain comparable properties you had to expand the search to a 20 mile radius around the subject property.

## Sales Price or List Price

Understanding the value of the subject property is often determined by the sale prices of the recent comparable or the current list prices of the comparable properties. These values are before you make adjustments but are still important for the BPO recipient to see. Absolute prices irrelevant of adjustments gives a feel for the range people have paid for comparable properties. Whether the comparable properties are identical or not, it helps give a feel of the recent sold figures and current competition.

## Data Source

Many BPO requestors will want to know the source your data. There are multiple sources of data but the most common answers to this question are MLS (multiple listing service) or Tax (tax records). Some data may appear in the tax records that weren't necessarily sold through the MLS so you may be able to find more comparables from the tax records. With the understanding that you may be able to find additional sales, it's important to consider that these sales may not be arm's length transactions.  An arm's length transaction is one in which neither party has a relationship and have acted independently in the sale.  Sometimes an estate sale or sale to a child may be recorded in the tax records but not a fair indication of value given a parent may have sold a home under value to their child or any other reason.

## Sales Date and DOM or Days on Market

How long has a property been on the market, or has it already sold?  If it sold, when was the sale date and how long was the property on the market (DOM)?  The most recent closed or settled comparable is the most relevant closing as its closest to the current market conditions.  How long was a property marketed for?  Maybe a property received top dollar but it was marketed for 365 days.  If the seller or property owner is not interested in waiting a year to sell a property they will have to consider this.  How long have the active listings been marketed for.  Maybe the closed sales sold very quickly but suddenly the market has changed and the listed comparables have been on the market for an extended period of time.  These factors and times help decide the market value.  Adjustments can be made either way for this assuming very short list times may mean the property was underpriced whereas longer DOM timeframes may mean the property was overpriced.

There are some cases where a bank or client may order a BPO for a historical date. Maybe they are auditing a file or application and they want to know what the value of a property was at a particular date in the past. You would look to obtain closed comparables from closest to that time period as possible but not after the date provided.

## Sales or Financing Concessions

When inventory was at an all-time high and sales had slowed dramatically, many institutional sellers found they had to try and sweeten the deal in an effort to make their properties more appealing. REO properties or bank owned sales often were not updated. Some of the larger banks and often Real Estate Developers will offer incentives to make the homes more appealing. Examples of this may be 6 months of Association Dues paid by the seller or 3% credit towards closing costs or a golf membership with the purchase of a home. These incentives have value and should be considered when comparing properties to one another. If one seller paid for closing costs on the sale of a home, the comparable would need to be adjusted accordingly to accurately reflect that.

## Location, Location, Location

As you have heard many times before, the most important characteristic of any home is its location. The location is the most important factor in valuing a property. This is a common field in most BPO reports and can be utilized in a variety of ways. The location may be used to indicate one property is up against train tracks when the others are interior lots. It may be used to define one property as being on a cul-de-sac where the others are on main streets. It can be used to state the name of the community a property is in whereas the comparables may be in neighboring communities. All of these factors, which are essentially related to the location are important to the value of a property and making appropriate adjustments.

## Ownership Type

There are a number of different ways to convey property and these variations in ownership have a huge impact on the value of the property. The most common conveyance and the highest ownership interest possible is Fee Simple ownership. While this is the most common type of ownership in America, there are other options like Leasehold or Co-op ownership. Leasehold ownership means that you are leasing the right to occupy or own the property for a fixed period of time. This is often found in the extent of 99 year land leases. Another type of ownership is the Cooperative. This is often found in larger cities or areas of higher density with large buildings. New York City has a large number of Co-op buildings, which are essentially an ownership of shares of a company that entitle you to use of a particular property. Regardless of the type of ownership the property is owned or sold with, it's important to make sure that your comparable properties are similar forms of ownership and if not, than appropriate adjustments are made for them.

## Site and View

While it may sound like site and view are similar attributes, these are often confused with one another. The truth is that they have nothing to do with one another. Site is actually referring to the plot of land or the parcel size. You may use acres or square feet in this field but make sure to use the same unit size across all of the comparable properties and subject so they can easily be compared with one another. If you are doing a BPO for a condominium this field may not be appropriate and can be left blank. Some townhomes however come with a little plot of land in front or back and that can be entered in this field as well.

View on the other hand is what you think it is. What is the view from the property? Do you have an ocean front view or a dumpster view? Is one property a garden view or eastern exposure and another property western exposure? What view is superior and what's the value of this? Sometimes views have minimal impact on properties but other times you can have as much as a 30% change in value in some buildings based on views from different sides of the building.

## Design, Appeal, Quality

There are often characteristics of a home or its architecture that make one home more appealing than another.  Home 1 may have the same statistical attributes as Home 2 in every way except in the design or the curb appeal.  If Home 1 was designed to look like a box and Home 2 was designed by a world renowned architect with interesting architecture and appeal, this is where it should be noted.  In addition to the appeal of the property, the quality of the construction is extremely important in areas of the country with natural disasters.  Is the home made of concrete block and hurricane resistant or is it wood frame and susceptible to the big bad wolf blowing it down.  This is where it should be reflected.

## Year Built

The year that homes are built in various parts of the country is often an indication to the type of construction, quality of construction and other factors.  For example in parts of California and Florida homes that were built in 2005 and 2006 often had problems with defective drywall (aka Chinese Drywall) and buyers when comparing homes to one another the age of construction is an important indicator. Adjustments should be made for the age of the property but you shouldn't always assume that an older home is less desirable than a newer home.  In many parts of the country, historically preserved homes may sell at a premium to newer constructed homes and these nuances of the market are for you to show in this area.

## Condition

Overall the condition of the property can probably be summed up into a couple of terms.  Excellent, Good, Fair, Poor.  Some institutional clients may have specific coding systems that they would prefer you to use but the four types provided are the most widely accepted.  While you may not have had access to the interior of all these properties, you can often see pictures in the MLS or you can read descriptions.  This should give you an idea of the condition enough to make an estimate.  If you have details about the comparables and their conditions you can make more detailed adjustments.  If you don't have details then you are better served by not making large adjustments based on a hunch.  Like usual the more data and information you can provide the better.

## Room Counts and Living Area

Just about all BPO formats have a section to itemize and breakdown room counts.  Some have sections for total amounts of rooms and bedrooms and bathrooms.  Some allow you to detail subgrade or basement rooms and bathrooms.  In addition to rooms you will be asked to provide the Gross Living Area.  Sometimes it's Gross Living Area and Under Air Square Footage.  These are all straight forward values that you can determine from the MLS, tax records and observation.

Some things to consider when making adjustments is that often tax records are inaccurate. Either square footage is outdated or room counts may be off as people have converted rooms or divided rooms. You will have to rely on the best information you have at the time to report this information but it's extremely important not to double adjust in this section. If you are making an adjustment based on square footage then you may not want to make another adjustment for the bedroom count.

Opinions differ somewhat, but generally speaking when you have made an adjustment for the square footage then it may not make sense to make the same adjustment again for an additional bedroom. Let's look at another example to see where the confusion is. In the example below we have our subject property and then we have a comparable sold property with one less bedroom and 500 less square feet. If we take the sales price of Comparable Sold 1 of $100,000 and divide it by the square feet Comparable Sold 1 we get an approximate value of $67 per SqFt of value. With this approximation we could merely take the difference of the two properties square footage and multiple it by this valuation.

**Subject Property Square Footage – Comparable Sold 1 Square Footage = 2000 – 1500 = 500 SqFt**

**500 SqFt x $67 per SqFt = $33,500**

While this is a linear approach to calculating the valuation difference it may not be a fair valuation. Is the Subject really worth $33,500 more than the Comparable. This is a matter of opinion but it's probably unfair to take a straight line approach like this to adjust the difference. Someone clearly would pay more for the additional square footage but probably not $33,500 more. Let's assume they are willing to pay $15,000 more for the property. Once again the comparable is inferior so we add money. This means we make and adjustment of adding $15,000.

| | Subject Property | Comparable Sold 1 | Adjustments |
|---|---|---|---|
| Address | 123 Elm Street | 125 Elm Street | $0 |
| Sold Price | | $100,000 | |
| Square Feet | 2000 Square Feet | 1500 Square Feet | $15,000 |
| Bed/Bath | 3 Beds / 3 Baths | 2 Beds / 3 Baths | ? |
| | | Adjusted Value | ? |

Now that we have settled on a $15,000 difference for the square footage let's consider the bedroom and bathroom count. The subject property has 3 bedrooms and the comparable sold property has 2 bedrooms. Clearly the additional bedroom is valuable and should be accounted for, but wait, we have already made an adjustment to the home based on the difference in square footage. This difference theoretically takes into account this additional bedroom and should we take a similar linear approach of adding the value for another bedroom we arguably would be double adjusting for it.

Not so fast. There are two schools of thought here, but this is generally the reasoning behind making at least some adjustment. Many people believe that if you have made the adjustment in square footage then no further adjustment should be made in the bedroom count. Here is the problem with that theory. Let's assume both homes had the identical square footage. They both had 2000 square feet but one home had 2 bedrooms and one had 3 bedrooms. Clearly the home with 3 bedrooms would be more desirable for most purchasers. They have identical square footage but an additional bedroom. That means that there is a value to a bedroom count outside of the additional square footage it may or may not add to a property. With this reasoning you should make an adjustment for the bedroom count but do so with the understanding that you are merely adjusting for the added benefit of the bedroom and not the potential square footage it may add.

It really depends on the market you are in but for the sake of this example let's say its $5,000. Once again, the comparable is inferior so we are adding to its value.

| | Subject Property | Comparable Sold 1 | Adjustments |
|---|---|---|---|
| Address | 123 Elm Street | 125 Elm Street | $0 |
| Sold Price | | $100,000 | |
| Square Feet | 2000 Square Feet | 1500 Square Feet | $15,000 |
| Bed/Bath | 3 Beds / 3 Baths | 2 Beds / 3 Baths | $5,000 |
| | | Adjusted Value | $120,000 |

Based on these adjustments it now appears that the subject property is worth about $120,000 based on the fact that it's larger and has an additional bedroom.

## Functional Utility

Sometimes people modify homes or build things specifically suited to them that may not make sense for the majority of purchasers. For example maybe the prior homeowner wanted to have access to their garage directly from their master bathroom or maybe they preferred to enter from the rear of their property so they closed up the front door and foyer to make another bedroom and put the main access into the home at the rear. These are examples of items that may affect the functional utility of a home. Some people believe that this area should be entered merely with a yes or no and then adjusted and others feel that an Excellent, Good, Fair, Poor rating may be more appropriate. It is really up to you, which scale you would like to use and then use it to adjust accordingly. If you are making adjustments in these fields you should absolutely explain the reasoning in the comments section of the BPO.

## Heating and Cooling or Energy Efficient Items

More and more homes are being built with various energy efficient characteristics including alternate methods of heating and cooling homes. Some homes work with central air while others may just have a fireplace for heating. The details of the heating and cooling solutions as well as any energy efficient characteristics should be noted in this area. The value of central air conditioning compared to window units can have a substantial change in value of a property. Other examples are solar powered water heaters or energy efficient windows. These items can be costly and are valuable to the home as a whole.

## Garage and Carport

Does the property offer a carport or garage and the comparables don't have one. While this may seem like a trivial adjustment, there are areas of the country where parking sells for up to $100,000 for a spot. If a condo comes with one parking spot as opposed to two assigned spots it may be a decision maker or breaker for many purchasers. This space on the BPO should be used to detail the differences. Covered Parking, Garage, 2 Car, Carport, Assigned, Deeded, Valet all are acceptable values for this field based on the situation of the particular property.

## Porches, Decks, Patios, Balconies, Pools, Fireplaces, Fences, Lions and Tigers oh My.

There are often sections towards the end of the adjustments on the BPO for adjustments of various features that have not been covered in the traditional adjustment areas. This gives you the flexibility to call out features that the subject or comparable may have that differentiates it from the other homes. Maybe the subject has a fenced yard and none of the comparables have fences and it's important to adjust for the value this provides. There are countless variables that could be accounted for here and it's really up to you as real estate professional to include those that have an effect on values. If the features don't have an effect on value it's less important to include.

## Repairs

Repairs is often a difficult section for many real estate professionals. This section is extremely important to itemize all of the repairs that you can see from your inspection of the property. While you may not be a certified contractor or inspector, there are many repairs and problems that are noticeable on your walkthrough. You will want to reference your photos to make sure you have itemized all repairs. Your objective here is to outline all of the repairs required to bring the property back into good condition. It's important to understand you are not necessarily recommending these repairs. This is merely to provide a comprehensive list all required repairs.

Some homes may not have power or running water when you have access to them and it's important to note this in the comments. You would be unable to determine the condition of the plumbing or electric systems without active utility accounts.

Once you have itemized the individual repairs you should provide what you believe is a rough cost to repair these items based on your professional experience. The client is aware that you are using estimates and that furthermore you can only report what's visible without having professional inspections and assessments completed. Some institutional clients may provide a unit cost or estimates for repairs that they would like to use but most of the time the figures are coming from your rough estimates. Remember, the pricing is wholesale. All of the repairs you are noting in a BPO report should equal the total value of the difference in condition between a property in average condition and the subject property.

## Marketing Strategy and Comments

Arguably the marketing strategy and comments section of any BPO is the most important part. The majority of your BPO is used to show a mathematical approach to showing the value of the property based on outside conditions, property condition, competitive sales, and current condition. The problem with this statistical data is that it does a poor job of painting the overall picture. These sections are where you as a real estate professional need to bring it all together to best describe the property, its condition, the market, and your recommendations for marketing the property. Below are a list of questions you can ask yourself and make sure you are addressing in your comments section. Once again you are a local professional and the client may be in another country with no prior knowledge to the home.

## Questions to Address in Comments

- Is property marketable the way it is?
- If it's not marketable what repairs would you recommend be completed?
- Is there a particular repair you would like to elaborate on?
- Who is the most likely purchaser for this property?
- Are there security concerns with the property that should be addressed immediately?
- Did anything catch you as unusual on your inspection of the property?
- Do you have any outside information about the neighborhood, community, city, or home that would important to a potential homebuyer?
- Did you make any adjustments that you would like to discuss or explain further that may appear counterintuitive on first glance?
- What are the positives of the property?
- What are the negatives of the property?
- Does the property have any particular violations, zoning, easement or encroachment concerns?

## Market Value

Now you have completed your BPO and provided an elaborate love story about the home.  It's time to value the home. Everything you have done up to this point is ultimately to determine a valuation of the property.  Different BPO's provide different value requests but generally they ask for a combination of the following figures.  Not all BPO's have all of these fields but below is a list to explain what they may ask for.

- **As Is Value** - What is the property currently worth?
- **As Is Suggested List Price** - What price would you list the property for now in its current condition.
- **Quick Sale Value** – What price would sell the home ASAP? This is also considered the fire sale value.
- **As Is Expected Sales Price** - What do you believe the property will actually sell for.
- **Repaired Value** – If the repairs you have outlined in the BPO were completed, what do you believe the property would be worth?
- **Repaired Suggested List Price** – If the repairs were completed what would you recommend the list price be for this property.
- **Repaired Expected Sales Price** – If the property was repaired and listed what do you believe the ultimate sales price would be.

When providing your As Is Value it's important to make sure that your value falls within the adjusted

range of your sold comparable.  Once you have
made all the adjustments to the comparable you
have arguably adjusted to make those properties
identical to the subject.  This means that the value
of the subject should fall within that range.  As an
example, if your adjusted values are $100,000 for
comparable sale 1, $150,000 for comparable sale 2
and $175,000 for comparable sale 3, your adjusted
range would be $100,000 to $175,000.


Recommended list price is based on your opinion
and your current market conditions.  There are
some markets where listing the property under its
current value often results in a bidding war with
offers and may result in selling the property for
more than it may be worth.  If this approach is
relevant in your market this is where you would
recommend the list price and make sure to
comment on your strategy in the comments section
of the BPO.


Repaired values is a debatable area.  As a real
estate professional you are aware that every dollar
spent on repairs doesn't ensure that it will add a
dollar to the value of the property.  The problem
here is that many Institutional clients ask that you
make sure that the repaired value of the property
equal at least the sum of the as-is value plus the
sum of repairs costs.


Clients often want to see the following:

## As Is Value + Repair Costs + Potential Added Value = Repaired Value

Unfortunately this is not always a true equation and you may spend $10,000 in plumbing repairs only to improve the value of the property $5,000.
Whether you agree or not with either approach it's important to know that you may be asked to justify or explain your numbers if they don't fall within this formula. Use the comments and explain yourself if you feel strongly enough about it.

Lastly it's important to understand that a BPO is by definition a Broker Price Opinion. This is your opinion of the value. You may be asked to explain your reasoning or your adjustments or how you came to your valuation but ultimately it's your opinion. If you feel strongly about your opinion than you can always stand by it. Don't be pressured to adjust the figures to match a report or appraisal or other pressures from outsiders. Your opinion is your opinion and you want to be able to stand by it.

**Photos**

Photos are an important part of any BPO. Always keep in mind that the party reviewing / requesting the BPO report is often in a completely different part of the country then where the property is located. You are playing the role of their eyes and ears in the field.

When performing an exterior BPO you will not have access to the interior of the property and therefore cannot take interior pictures. Exterior photos should include a picture of the street the home is situated on. The purpose of this picture is to illustrate a heavily trafficked street or other potential defects to the subject's location. Exterior photos of the subject property should include a picture from each side of the home as well as the front yard from as many angles as possible. Take as many pictures as you can while you are at the property. Nothing is worse then getting back to the office only to realize that you forgot to take a picture of the right side of the home.  A commonly requested photo for an exterior BPO is address confirmation. The requestor would like photographic proof of the house numbers. If you cannot find numbers on the house, do not stress it, take pictures of the mailbox or any other numbered items that can assist in identifying the home.

When tasked to complete an interior BPO you should take the same photos you would for an exterior BPO, however, additionally take photos of the interior of the home. Each room in the home should be photographed. Each item that you feel requires repairs should also be documented in a photograph. With digital cameras there is no additional cost associated with taking as many photographs as possible. You do not want to get back to the office to realize that you are missing a picture of the kitchen damage you remember seeing. If you have too many photos you can always delete the extras, unfortunately, the inverse is not true.

As a side note, you will want to adjust the settings on your camera to take the smallest images possible. Most digital cameras today have default settings that produce very large images, which are important when you are going to print an image. For the purpose of a BPO, you will want to have an image that is visible, however, you do not need to have an extremely large image. In many cases your client will not want extremely large file sizes. Check your cameras instruction manual for more instructions on customizing the image size.

Smart phones are also a popular choice for BPO photos. One caveat to using a smart phone camera is the sometimes slow processing time and the limited flash. If you are just getting started in the BPO business using a smart phone camera initially may make sense before investing in a digital camera.

**Thank You**

Hopefully this has clarified some of the confusion with BPOs and you feel more comfortable providing your value for properties. Remember there is no right or wrong answer. A property is worth what someone is willing to pay for it and on any given day that's a different number.  To get a free list of BPO companies to register with you can go to http://www.bpoforms.com/blog/how-to-complete-a-bpo